Kingsway

Kingsway

MICHAEL TURNER

ARSENAL PULP PRESS
VANCOUVER

Arsenal Pulp Press
103-1014 Homer Street
Vancouver, B.C.
Canada v6b 2w9

The publisher gratefully acknowledges the assistance of the Canada Council and the Cultural Services Branch, B.C. Ministry of Small Business, Tourism and Culture.

Art direction by Dean Allen
Cover photo courtesy of the Vancouver Public Library
Author photo by Judy Radul
Printed and bound in Canada

CANADIAN CATALOGUING IN PUBLICATION DATA

Turner, Michael, 1962-
Kingsway

Poems.
ISBN 1-55152-028-1

1. Kingsway (Vancouver, B.C.) – Poetry. I. Title.
PS8589.U7485 1995   C811'.54   C95-910824-6
PR9199.3.T87K5 1995

Table of Contents

Acknowledgements

Titles of the poems in "Kingsway: A re: Development Project" are lines taken from the following poems or books, in order of appearance:

"Lap Top," by Jeff Derksen
"Scrim," by Kathryn MacLeod
PulpLog, by Barry McKinnon
"Idio-Mantic," by Roy Miki
"Chronicles," by Judy Radul
"Door Matter," by Gerry Gilbert
"Resumé," by Gerald Creede
Link Fantasy, by Stan Douglas and Deanna Ferguson
"Billy Joe Royal," by Maxine Gadd
"A Tall Tale," by Phyllis Webb
"Stop," by Robin Blaser
Across the Street, Across the River & Over the Mountain,
     by Neil Eustache
"Discourse," by Sharon Thesen
"The Difference Three Makes: A Narrative," by Daphne Marlatt
"Thimking Of You," by Dan Farrell
"Bitterness: In Teen Taal (Sixteen-Beat Rhythm Cycle),"
     by Phinder Dulai
"From a Translation of the *Carmina Burana*," by Catriona Strang
"Waiting for a Ride Out of Here," by Evelyn Lau
"Farewell To Wheeler Without Saying Goodbye,"
     by Tom Wayman
"This Story," by Dorothy Trujillo Lusk
A Sunday Drive, by Lisa Robertson and Nancy Shaw

Thanks to Dean Allen, Lynn Crosbie, Dan Farrell, Deanna Ferguson, Brian Lam, and Judy Radul

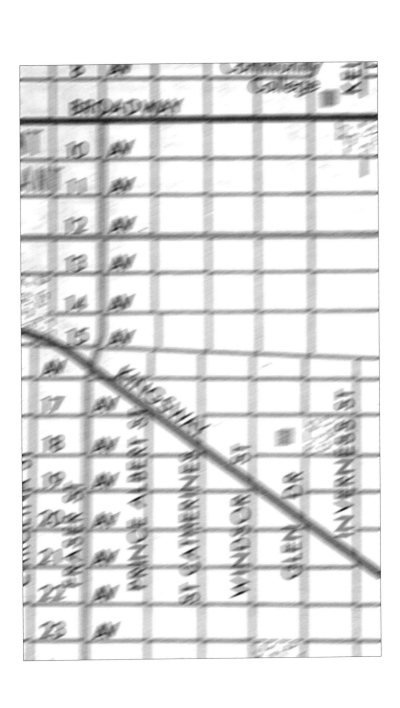

For Judy

1

KINGSWAY

1 a.m. this road, this way
diagonal, in opposition
2 the grid, the monarchy
of streets: Beatrice, Sophia
3 princes, Earles, a Duchess, lords
& ladies waiting at
45 degrees with soldiers, explorers
businessmen, saints
6 places in Australia, a Salish
name that means "people of many names" from
7th to 10th Avenues, indefinitely
a taxi driver drives the whole
8 miles with a carload
of offshore investors
9 times before giving up
looking for the historic Gladstone Inn
10 hours later swerving to
avoid a fallen man sleeping off

the bottle, broken, wakes up, swearing: where
pink neon meets a robin's egg blue pick-up
truck yellow caution meets a single/white/male
meets a single/Chinese/family flowers at the Esso
meeting cardboard from the McDonald's and the staff
meeting at the 7-11 meet money stolen from
the Safeway near the broken horn of a Dodge
Ram inches from the back of the #19
bus advertising ground meats two dollars a pound
or one hundred dollars a half-hour meeting the pedestrian
crossing stop red hand-job-to-mouth comes-to-go white man
stars leaves meeting a deep blue summer night sky meeting
black smoke from the funeral home meets the streets
meeting avenues like King Ed, drives like Victoria, ways
like me

(iii)

hyphen-like
like slashes/dashes – a series of
broken   staggered   lines
paralleling apostrophic storefronts
crumbling under an old code
of paint, semi-gloss, semi-colon-
ized by retired white-wall kicking
car salesmen: have ize got a deal fer you
they said: the British cleared the way
to link the navy in the inlet
with the business of New West

now people get on
just to get off

this row(ed), the sway:

the first way
  the short-cut
   the clear-cut
    the back door
     the quick route
      the mud bath
       the milk-run
        the boardwalk
         the bored walk
          the low-rise
           the highway
            the stagecoach
             another stage
              the pit-stop
               the piss-stop
                the piss-up
                 the line-up
                  the gateway
                   the safe way
                    the drive-in
                     the drag-strip
                      the strip-tease
                       the hand hold
                        the back-hand
                         the cheap rent
                          the one-stop
                           the car-wash
                            the drive-by
                             the get-away
                              the get-a-life
                               the fuck-up
                                the low-down
                                 the no way
                                  the low way
                                   the buy low
                                    the hell hole
                                     the good buy

car radios report:
news/weather/sports
traffic/editorial
the first trucks
of the new day
are yesterday's trucks
from Prince George, Prince Rupert
Penticton, the States
their gross weight
an exercise
in considering
their cargo:
2-by-4s
of Douglas fir
fur coats made
of beaver, bear
mink, seal
sealed palates
of minced salmon
containers of
office supplies like
waybills, staples
bags of briquettes
for barbecues
canisters of artificial
flavour for snow cones
boxes of cold medicines
shivering at a stop
light, idling

their weight
waits for the light
of day, the first trucks
of the new day wait
for a moment
to consider that
if everything else on earth
including earth itself
were loaded into these trucks
would they float
lighter than returning
empty tomorrow
to Prince George, Prince Rupert
Penticton, the States?

(vi)

on the way, wayward:
cars out-numbering trucks
from 10:00 a.m. to 1:00 p.m.
10:1 as the morning drive
becomes a tape: music or self-
improvement as the news by now
has been determined as the weather's
been predicted as teams move up & down
the standings as editorials form as drops of
rain dot the hood as the bus comes & goes
east to Metrotown, west to downtown as
taxis rush and trucks begin to up their
number as the tape hiss becomes
rain hiss as what was dropped
off is now picked up as what
was started is now refinished
as news is newer as weather
is never accurate as teams
are just getting under-
way as editorials are
standing by

(vii)

And now this. They don't know what they have here. Just look. If they think we're gonna take it, then we better be better paid. Look what happened at Kingsgate Mall. You can tell where they're at by the decline in their Santa Clauses. An Eaton's instead of a Saan. And we've got a SkyTrain stop. Like, my friends down at VLC Properties. Like, just the other day. I don't wear a suit for nothing, you know. And I'm sure as hell not gonna wear one just to go to church at these prices. I'm making good money for the first time in my life without moving. And it's gonna stay that way.

(viii)

dates & addresses
do not correspond:
a letter sent to 1913
will not be opened
because it won't be
received, however:
on October 1, 1913
the opening of what
was already open
the making new of what
was already known
as Westminster Road
formerly the New Road
the Black Trail before that
the False Creek Trail before
that something without
documentation, papers
they say down at archives:
we simply don't know:
a Native trail, certainly
not a road, though
beavers, a few bear
sightings, no signs of
occupation, not much
more than a place for
subsistence collection
a No Man's Land, a path-
way if you want, then

(ix)

History. So time, then. Place, too. An intersection
where a small girl was struck down by a team of horses.
This may have happened, but there are no records
of it happening. But let's just say it did, then, 'cause
it probably did. Odds are that it did. There were
children everywhere. There always have been. And
teamsters running rough-shod, sliding back and forth
a hundred times a day in the November mud. Pissed up
and off at the Gladstone or Junction Inns. Yes, it is
November. Yes, they are drunk. Yes, she is dead.
History. Then. Too.

(x)

the esqueness, the likeness
we bear to our -self, driving
at night with the lights off to see
where the light standards do
without us, but still with-
in visibility through a limited
number of just-misses
attracted to what's being present-
ed by its own glow, being all things
to some choices: a nickname
change in mid-career from
Nick to Ed, from 9th Avenue
to Broadway the cop makes a con-
vincing actor, the grocer almost
grosses a million, the clerk used
to be a cleric – yet all of them
carry on as if they were or weren't
counting on each finger is digital
suffix it to say: the endings justify
the meanings

2

15 POEMS ABOUT KINGSWAY

I am now that you are
reading this and that
this is not being read
to you
thinking this will never be
read at a reading
this will be read
as driving is
reading not driven
the writing not the written
the plot destination
the stanza blocks
the light punctuation
you will go to
your getting for-
get even getting
this is not being read
to you
thinking this will always be
driving the reading

it is written
in white paint
behind
the Sunshine Plaza
that Sarajeeni R.
likes it from
behind
the Sunshine Plaza
the word is
indistinguishable
after the word
from
though no one
notices anymore
even though
they've seen it
so many times
they used to
think the word
after from
was beyond
and if asked
again most people
would stick with beyond
although some would
argue be kind

3

in Canada
30 years
and a small business
later 5 children 5 grand-
children and still no
trace of the first-person
conjugation of the verb
to be
nor the ability
to read or write
nor the desire
to learn to speak
but in love
with life a maker
of objects the one one
goes to for their passport
photo in any language

4

taxi at Swanguard
is a Checker
the driver Lorenzo
takes a pass
on a fare
opens *L'Eco d'Italia*
news from home
though he's never
been there yet
he heads
to the page
where he reads
who scored
the winning goal
for Parma
enthusiastically
the crowd roars
the one-one goal
at Swanguard

5

at karaoke
up comes *You Light Up My Life*
and behind you with you
in it is Venice
you're staring at a gondola
as it cuts through the brown waters
of the canal the gondolier dressed
in a shirt you're admiring
the words are beginning
to appear on the screen
and you're not singing them
for some reason you think
you can't see them
because you forgot your glasses
even though you don't wear glasses
someone in the audience
is beginning to hum the melody
inserting words now
to carry on
you turn to the audience
and notice there are twenty more
people than when you got up
to stand in front of and in Venice
a strong baritone is now
rising from his chair arms out like Lanza
and people are looking at him
smiling and nodding their approval
thinking he would be easier
to look at and listen to

if he were standing in front of
and in Venice
and that you would be
watching anonymously
with them

6

she'll get shit-
kicked for it but
for only four fives
and a ten she blew
him anyway she says
and then again says
they take advantage
of their own weirdness
they won't go to bank machines
and get the cash
right once they've talked
business we gotta go now
and do it right now
and that's all I got so
there in the parking lot
of the Value Village
she had clothes on
she bought there
she remembers the white
tank-top on the rack
he pushed his hand down
the other turning
up the Canucks' game
she had to pull his cock
out or he couldn't
get it on he said get it
hard her face
pressed hard against
the steering wheel

him fat in her mouth
toilet paper bits stuck
under the foreskin licking
the sticky head smooth
shit is it thick
mouth corners crack
more little bits is
just where the money is

overheard
at Wally's Burgers
then a pushing
match lit dimly
in the parking lot
said it's a free
country no it's
not don't give a fuck
for under this amount
your fries are ready
Eddie but no one
answers the call
the cops arrive too
late they just wait
and take names
an Edna but no Eddie
there's some blood
some grease
taken for analysis
your burger's ready
and two people look up
and are handcuffed
for not talking
the brightest pink
turban someone's
overheard to say

8

it wasn't the money so much
as the opportunity to make
money the way they wanted to make
money and the way they wanted
to take some of the money
they made in other ways
and make it legal that
they opened a laundromat
and a restaurant and a video store
next to other laundromats
and restaurants and video stores
that the problems started
the nasty looks the heavy language
physical violence and death
and the money made by
promising that that would go away
so more money made
in other ways
until those laundromats
and restaurants and video stores
sold out to the neighbouring
laundromats and restaurants
and video stores
who then closed down
those stores and left them
closed

the day after Canada Day
sale at Lumberland
couples contractors artists
mingling by the wood stacks
our country keeps coming up
disagreement as to how old
we are now how many feet
we'll need how polite we are
compared to Americans
how much custom-
cutting costs the forests
a car parked for every tree now
fir and cedar when Canada was
invented out here the oldest road
in Vancouver was already here
when Expo came to town
that B-class world expo-
sition with a transportation
theme Skytrain praised
by florists and car salesmen alike
as the future in a city fortunate
enough to have bypassed free-
ways how lucky we were supposed
to be Expo made no celebration
of Vancouver's oldest road
how this road's six years older
than Canada even older than
Vancouver talk turns back
to our country with a new

enthusiasm when mention is made
of our most recent enemies to date
Somalia Spain for sure that's two
somebody brings up the fur trade
somebody's happy just to be hated
consensus on hatred when talk re-
turns to freeways

the art student
referred to as
the student
of the art college
by the Brownings
the landlords
hadn't been heard
from since Easter
sensing they'd
disappeared
the art student
crawled in
the kitchen window
of the Brownings' suite
looking for evidence
of foul play instead
woke up Mr. Browning
dozing on the couch
in his gaunch he was
a big man barely five-six
but over two-twenty
holding the picture frame
where their wedding day went
her teapot not
in its usual place
on the sideboard
below the painting
of the Brownings
by the student
of the art college

in the seventh inning
his station wagon pulled up
just past centre-field
white with a missing window
the other team was batting
he was wearing a white
Arrow short-sleeve looking
like that actor in the civil rights
movie glasses dark pants
and the kid at bat wallops it
between left- and centre-
and out he runs waving
his megaphone and grabs
the rolling ball and starts
shouting at my son at first
it sounded like retching then
you could make out little bits
he was clearly American
from the south a Christian
going on about coming back
to Jesus and stuff for maybe
oh ten seconds when finally one
of the coaches hits him on
the third try with a baseball
in the gut he goes down
doubles over the kids
in tears running all over
the place the parents
held him down 'til you came

Christ it's only Little League
nothing like this ever happened
when we were young

what looks like Vietnamese
to you is just English
in reverse a bankruptcy
or it's backwards
in the rear-view
what was once a Safeway
is now the flea market
though no less productive
it contains no produce
not much different except
the lighting is lower
so darkness for sale then
what are people reading
when asked at the D.Q.?
one guy responds
some whitey from somewhere
you arrive at Apollo
to pick up a muffler
you pick it up alright
then hand it back
to the man who'll install it
when you feel like dancing
it's been years since
they danced there
when they called it the High-Hat
before that the Gladstone

small town language
writers of community
newspapers small
towns Lokchong
Hatinh Simla
Cranbrook even smaller
to minds only
accustomed to small
neighbourhoods
in the big city
Royal Oak Edmonds
Middlegate Kensington
small but long
on names sitting at small
tables writing in long-
hand on the side besides
doing immigration credit
union mufflers produce
whose marriage death
opinion conviction
a new book on literacy
to be launched
at a community
centre there
will be food and drink
photographs television
people from community
cable someone to
monitor children
as they watch on
the monitors

14

small town language
writers of community
newspapers new
editorial slams
certain word usage
claiming their meaning
is rooted in small
towns not the big city
they're writing in
provides no examples
just keeps repeating
a dislike for
small town language
creeping in when pushed
gets up about the fact
that newspapers
inform and unfamiliar
words could just cloud
issues points to
the building of Metrotown
how important it was
to stick to the language
of the press releases
from government
developers
if it were to mean
anything at all
to future citizens
of Metrotown

Metrotown poetry
reading sing-song
the merchants hoped
said poets would
be fun on the con-
course but lively
ones funny poets
who would get
customer attention
like circus barkers
clowns blowing up
helium balloons
miming a face-painter
a salesman suggested
one poet should be
fired a bad attitude
didn't want their face
painted couldn't
write on the balloons
wouldn't perform
above a whisper

3

KINGSWAY:
A RE: DEVELOPMENT
PROJECT

It's Cold for a Description

1-A and am all
ways here
is my place
now for all time
there the lights change
nothing moves
the passer-by
is a black cloud
before a blue sky
and the yellow light
in behind
how they are
up there when
all is what is
down here
in yesterday's snow
a gridlock
an accident
to wave a hand over
and make it not happen
the flashing red
of the ambulance
no need to pull
the sheet up
just let it fall
a robin's egg blue
pick-up truck
ran the yellow
skid marks pick up

black slashes
whatever was inside
dead and under
the body work rust
or blood

The Man's Body Hit the Lamppost
Ten Feet in the Air

reporters arrive by taxi slowly
B C T V is stuck off Knight
someone from the flea market
has filmed the whole thing
testing a G A F super-8 camera
he'll sell it for the price he'll pay
for the camera he's just
an old man who likes doing things
fairly just an old man
from just past Penticton
the driver was teen-aged
he had drive-thru McDonald's
somebody writes: a Big Mac
was found two blocks away
how much for the film
that guy's got in his camera?
the C B C crew sets up
shots from the corner
a librarian asks if they'd not
block the door
a van pulls up with overdue books
somebody writes: the old man's name
is something like Rupert
we'll now take you live
to the scene of the accident
the sergeant in charge
is preparing a statement
bring me the man
with the super-8 camera
somebody writes: a story idea:
let's do something on overdue books

Against a Yawning Grave, a Piss-Hole in the Snow

St. Catherines St.
never-ending drive-by
a dog waits to cross
paws buried in snow
a seeing-eye dog
on leave
of its senses
itself lost
a short trip to Rip's
a shepard-lab cross
paws melting the snow
an ambulance soft
slow to St. Joseph's
there's no need to hurry
backs up and barks
pausing in new snow
steam off the pink tongue
returns to its master
hands in its notice

The Idea of a Street

EVERYTHING MUST GO
so you go
NEXT YEAR'S MODELS IN NOW
so you drive by
and like the red one
it makes you hungry
so you DRIVE THRU
to the line up
TRY OUR BACON DOUBLE-CHEESE
so you try one
'cause you're like that
as you drive out
thinking I'D LIKE TO TEACH THE WORLD TO SING
and you drive on
humming IN PERFECT HARMONY
as you drive past
GARAGE SALE
you make a u-turn
NO U-TURN
and you drive back
singing IT'S THE REAL THING
a Coke sign
and you're like that

And Sad Sorrow Walks My Salary

the billboard campaign
its ad verse now not copy
the logo the product the text
all suggest poetry as
an organizational model
a navigable way of arriving at
living the game's at 5:00 p.m.
so wearing your 501s will make you
late though not expected
the face is the first thing you'll see
it's what's being called your performance
the mouth will open a fraction of a
second before the first word is heard
please do not attempt a lip read
just keep your head bowed down
and be thankful that the product's
available that no one will tell you
that not only can you not afford
the purchase but that you are
wholly unworthy of selling it
this will not be the first time this
will happen you will have
felt this shame before

The Moment Takes No Time At All

the taste could be better
described if it wasn't
called an imperial roll
but a roll-call
a Ho Chi Minh
roll or a fall
of Saigon roll
or the CIA's
roll or under
corporate sponsorship
a Rolaids roll or
a Dow Chemical roll
whatever happened
to Esther Rolle
of *Good Times* fame?
that post-war-American-
black-ghetto-comedy-
drama roll
the French word
for roll or
the Chinese
the Cambodian
the Russian
or the comprador-
in-absentia roll
or the escaped-with-
their-lives roll
or the idea-of-
Marguerite Duras

roll the rock'n'
roll war roll
the fuck-you-G.I.
Bill roll
or our roll
the peacekeeper's roll
more Canadians daily
swearing-in to a queen
so now more than ever
Canada's roll

His Life a Series of Small

ate the chips
and tested positive
they want the award back
the coveted Acorn
the publisher's furious
demanding a recount
more blood was taken
for the Canada Council
a company statement
and calls to the jury
word is that Purdy
will send in a letter
a consensus is building
he'll send in a y
there's a party at Scott's
and no doubt the topic
will be picking you up
if you're ready for people

Sit Down. Look Up.
Make Notes for Antiquity

something rising up
where the car lot was one
more thing than just one
thing for sale there now
MetroVista advertises
condos retail shops
but no view of Metro
unless downtown is Metro
a better view of Kingsgate
though the view of MetroVista
is best from behind inside
the Western Front upstairs Eric goes
they're pile-driving they're pile-driving
have to pile-drive Kate says because
the soil's all loose where the creek once was
yes I know I know says Eric like Hank's
always saying let's bring back the creek
let's just bring it back better than just
a monument on Main Street that creek
turned the wheel of Doering's Brewery
that creek could just as easily turn
Alan Storey's wheel outside
the Western Front if it wasn't
for MetroVista in the way
when you're standing where
Westminster Road & 9th was

Keep on Moving, Billy Joe

back now but from where?
consecutive five year drug-
trafficking and possession
sentences a mountaintop
or a fixture in the labyrinth
that is Collingwood?
Billy Joe Royal mover-
and-shaker at the Circle Square
real estate bad-ass shaking
hands with a squatter
after selling the squatter's
home to VLC Properties
or Billy Joe Royal squatter
refusing to move instead
standing defiantly in the door
the megaphone aimed
at Billy it's okay Billy
just come on out slowly
and sign the release
Billy's holding
firm on the stoop no
way pigs no way you'll get me
moving my name's
Billy Joe Royal
and there's a lot more
out there where we come from

And Nested There, and
Nested There and Stayed

the concert unforgotten
walking from Stanley Park
via Chinatown for something
buzz or hunger the singer's
groovy pants faux English
accent eventually Broadway
the crowd down to you and
bill his lisping psilocybin sighs
it's unfamiliar but we're not
lost look the Biltmore's pink
piping's so beautiful let's
stop smoke this to take off
the edge have you heard
Pat Lowther's poem about
the Blue Boy let's walk there
heading south angular listing
to the left wait bill Simpsons'
in the distance we're miles
from Marine sunburst guitar
soloing again fuzz up a tone
to Am now crossing at Jesus
The Light of the World neon
the Church of Technocracy
miles as the crow flies bill
at Central Park disappears
to the other side of Boundary

Wanted So Much to Enter the Brightness

his was a '32 Ford
all hotted-up
painted the colour
of sky at noon light
blue body yellow sun
fire flaming back from
the front panels his given
name in quotations
Neil below his elbow
on the driver-side door
tells everyone he chose
those colours because
he's just up at night
now defending his
everything he says
his was a new car
a '55 Chev in town
for the car show
this man from Tacoma
way older than Neil was
his car had no name
except for the names of
sponsors motor oil
spark plugs shocks
brilliant logos in all
shapes and colours
delicately placed
against a black as night car

The Birds Fly Past in Sorrow,
Fly By in Sorrow

the second world war's
ending solved the problem
of space between gas
stations by quickly
inventing the used car
and of what to summon
as justification for cutting
down trees meant
the establishment
of used car lots
and of what to do with
the boys coming home
how to get them off guns
as a means of persuasiveness
meant getting them defending
the integrity of a broken-down car
like one salesman did who didn't
take his uniform off for two years
'cause he sold more cars
that way imagine how many
he would have sold with
his machine gun on
how much bigger
everything would be

Mercury Vapour Night Entranced

swingin' at the Hat
kickin' out those Yankee dances
Connie Lucas ripped her dress
but kept on hoppin'
mad for those Yankee dances
the jitterbug the jumpin' jive
crazy at the Hat
boom-boom-boom-boom-
boom-boom-boom at the Hat
singin' and a-reelin' and a-
movin' and a-groovin'
at the Hat at the Hat
Louie Craddock knows
those Yankee dances
every Saturday gets ready
early for the Hat
lays out his best
on the side of the bed
for the Hat for the Hat
boom-boom-boom-boom-
boom-boom-boom at the Hat
dairy boys yell hey where ya goin'
to Connie on the Sunday
Connie yells back well I'm not tellin'
but come Saturday night
you can find me at the Hat at the Hat
boom-boom-boom-boom-
boom-boom-boom at the Hat
at the Hat Louie grabs Connie

Connie grabs back the band
lays into the wickedest beat
the shivering ride of the cymbalist's
beat the simplest beat at the Hat
at the Hat the clarinet stutters
the trumpet is king Louie finds
air at the foot of his feet the bass
climbs each rung in impossible
heat Connie so strong she pulls
Louie to speed at the Hat
at the Hat at the Hat

This Is All About Framing

October chum are up-creek
Fatty Mope and Biddy cut
long switches Maude Mills
scoffed a ball of yarn Biddy
found some pin wire Zip Kent
twisted into hooks should do
bacon for bait though
Tecky Round says spawning chum
won't bite on meat better to kick
them out like brewery men do
at Doerings' for breakfast Mope says
he saw a teamster there pitchfork
a chum squeeze out the eggs
and eat them with his beer
he burped and it sounded
so loud you could smell it
downstream

Under the Trees Out of Their Shape

Jones' door heard to slam
open cow's head turns corner
bell scrapes dull huff
Jones returns to oil
door knocked closed
by new cow moo
mooing for Jones
Jones moos back
thinks this cow loves
me why me why not me?
crowded stage pulls up
Jones
I am Jones
or Joseph Jones
as I am
known yes
Janes is my name
I'll be driving
stage between
Vancouver and New West
I am acquainted with Garvin
Samuel Garvin
a man you once worked for
that is correct Mr. Janes
any relation to Black Jones
Mr. Jones?
no relation
oh
nice to meet you Janes

nice to meet you Jones
cow's flank turns corner
stage flickers away
through trees
bell makes a loud
knock and another moo
from Jones' herd

The Raving of Your Soul as Your Mind Unravels and You

to Henry's as promised
some laurel for the front
to run along the fence
or a rose bush would be nice
is red or yellow better?
his nursery's been so helpful
they planted our begonias
you don't regret returning?
Vancouver's getting bigger
his business is expanding
he'll be bringing in exotics
there's a quartet at the bandstand
we could walk there after supper
were you happier in London?
do you really miss your parents?
what about the home we've made?
we have the kindest neighbours
what kind of place is England?
you know it's going nowhere
next year there'll be promotions
we'll plant a rhododendron
you decide the colour
is red or yellow better?

Sated with Pure Purpose, as Absence

eight straight days of rain
then sun at noon
water now flush
with the sewer
grate at the crosswalk
reflecting up
on faces blank waiting
to walk one face thinks
of work one face thinks
of working light changes
pissing on the other
side of the street

Into Some Blue Place of Vanishing

too loud below to
hear its single-prop a
flock of words following
a Sunday of bargains
some factory outlet in
Central Burnaby so you
know they'll be coming
this way from downtown
East Van maybe Kits it's
only when the letters pass
before a cloud can you
make out the redness of
each word urgent as red
gets magic as the need
for discount carpet can
be to those inevitable
cars at the light

About What Constitutes a Line

median strip oasis
shopping bags full
but for forgotten
items bar soap and
fruit trucks in
the distance bluebells
in the cracks a heat-ripple
is distant up-close in
daytime neon
looks farther away
can't go back now that
the market's closing but
closing slowly is not yet
closed going back
now that the traffic's at
its fattest so what
was forgotten is for-
gotten again soap for
the tub and something
for dessert plastic bags
thin from bulk and heat
new poetry by Peter Culley
in a book in the bag
bulging its straight
spine's gonna poke
it all open unless
the sidewalk comes in time

Very Gravity of an Undertaking

tires rub wrinkles
into gummed over
tar grooves the road
collecting in eddies
pebbles of pavement
pushing out the occasional
upside-down bottle
cap star-like over stone
blocks exposed here
and there big grinning
horse teeth after hooves
once made mud of
hooves in the shape of
typewriter keys stepped
up the announcement
of name changes the
decision to pull out the
street-cars and repave
when the time comes

Anticipate. Our Drive
Doubles as a Device of Future

the map is useless
unfold it turn it once
to the left then again
to the right ripping it still
useless you can't
read it you won't
find Pearl or Cherry
that way you won't
find anyone around
to help you
either best to forget it
out here or get your
friends wholesalers
testing stations to
move back to
Prior Commercial Woodland
whatever
your left- and right-
turn choices will be
dead-ends
wrong moves they will
only further contribute to
your frustration where
your decision to do something
only compounds your sense
of abandon at best
do nothing make new
friends learn to use
the telephone better buy

stuff at the retail price so
the corner store can continue
and lease a new car every year
so you'll never have to
get it tested then
stop driving